My First Pizza Recipe book, characters, text and images ©2021 *My First Recipes*.
My First Recipes mark and logo, ™*My First Recipes*.
All rights reserved.
ISBN: 978-1-7368133-0-0 (hardcover)

My First Pizza Recipe

written by Danielle Clout

illustrated by Sue Mattero

Pizza is yummy!

Let's make some pizza for everyone!

First comes the dough.
You roll it out thin.

Maybe pick a fun shape to put the dough in!

A circle or square would be a good start.

But how 'bout a star, triangle or heart?

Next comes the sauce.
Spread it all around
the dough.

All the way to the edges, as far as it will go!

Sprinkle *FAST!*

Sprinkle SLOOOOW

You can pick out some toppings
and place them with care.

Some peppers? Some mushrooms?
Some spice if you dare!

In the oven it goes to melt all the cheese.

And crisp up that dough as much as you please.

When out of the oven, let it cool down a touch, before grabbing a slice...

...to enjoy oh so much.

www.ingramcontent.com/pod-product-compliance
Ingram Content Group UK Ltd.
Pitfield, Milton Keynes, MK11 3LW, UK
UKHW060125240426
12049UKWH00014B/162